BRACKNELL
A TOWN WITHIN THE GREAT WINDSOR FOREST

TERRY JOHN CLARK was born at number one Fairview Cottages, Bracknell. His family had resided in this house since 1908 when his great grandfather Bert Bickmore relocated from Slough.

Settled in Bracknell, Bert became the local blacksmith and his daughter Muld married a local man, Albert Earnest Sidney Clark, whom she'd known from school. Albert and Muld were married in December 1929 and in May 1930 their son Bernard Sidney Thomas Clark was born.

Bernard was bought up in the same cottage as his mother and attended Priestwood School as his parents had. When Bert died in 1950 Bernard bought forward his plans to marry Dorothy May Hobley and they too remained at the cottage. Terry was born into the family on the cold, frosty morning of 6 January 1953 and this was followed by the birth of his brother on 29 July 1957.

Terry had a happy upbringing in that cottage where he lived until 1967 when his mother and father bought a house in Wokingham. After 47 years Terry remains in this home yet his fond memories of Fairview Cottages prompted him to research and write this history of Bracknell town.

Bracknell

A TOWN WITHIN THE GREAT WINDSOR FOREST

Terry John Clark

SilverWood

Published in 2014 by SilverWood Books

SilverWood Books Ltd
30 Queen Charlotte Street, Bristol, BS1 4HJ
www.silverwoodbooks.co.uk

ISBN 978-1-78132-254-3

British Library Cataloguing in Publication Data
A CIP catalogue record for this book is available from
the British Library

Set in Sabon by SilverWood Books
Printed on responsibly sourced paper

To my father Bernard Sidney Thomas Clark

Contents

List of Illustrations	11
Pre-Roman Settlement	13
Roman Rule	15
Anglo-Saxon Rule	19
From Danish Kings to Norman Rule	23
The Middle Ages	27
The Tudors	31
The Stuarts and the Civil War	35
Easthampstead Park	37
Late 17th Century to Georgian Era	41
The Victorian Era	45
South Hill Park	47
The Victorian Bracknell Town	51
Lily Hill House	53
Wick Hill House	55
The Edwardians and the Great War	57
Mid-Twentieth Century	59
After World War II	63
Postscript	71

List of Illustrations

Lily Hill House 1880   73
George Canning 1881   73
Bracknell High Street 1907   74
Bracknell 1910   74
Church Road 1910   75
Frank Hobley 1918   75
George Littledale 1920   75
Bert Bickmore and Terry John Clark 1933   76
Easthampstead Park 1936   77
Old Bracknell c1950   77
New town houses 1951   78
Hinds Head pub 1965   78
Sidney Thomas Hobley 2003   79
Wick Hill House 2011   79

Pre-Roman Settlement

There is some evidence of early settlement at "Caesar's Camp", an Iron Age fortification and encampment settled by the Celts in 500 BC. The Celts were people from Southern European descent who arrived around 900 BC in Britain. The first wave of Celts did not stay long and were off across the sea to Ireland where they made a settlement. The second wave of Celts soon arrived and they became known as the Britannic Celts. They mingled with the native inhabitancy, people known as the Beaker Folk because of the strange bronze objects and pottery later found by an archaeologist. Those people crossed the ice from France to Britain before the end of the last Ice Age, but just 200 people made the trip. It is said that today we carry the DNA of those original people through the female line.

The Belgie tribe, who lived in "Caesar's Camp", had their base at Colchester where their king ruled over most of Southern Britain from 300 BC to about 43 AD. They were one of the most powerful Celt tribes in the country.

The arrival of Caesar and his armies in 55–54 BC did not disrupt life too much. They had silver and gold coinage and paid tribute to the great Roman leader, who stayed just over a year then left. He decided that the isles of Britannica were nothing more than an obscure backwater.

Nothing more was heard of the Romans for another 90 years. With the exception of trade, they carried on farming the area, making slow progress in warfare and the construction of tools. A coin was found in this area in the 15th century, dated 15–20 BC from the British King Cunobline. In 43 AD, a new Roman emperor decided to make a name for himself by invading Britannica and bring it into the Empire. This was Emperor Claudius, who needed a successful military campaign to establish his rule of the Empire, which he did in Britain within ten years. It became a province of the Empire at its most northern edge.

Roman Rule

From 100 AD, Caesar's Camp was suddenly completely abandoned. Why? Was it because of the poor farming lands surrounded by woods and forests? Or, was it the cold winters and hot summers recorded by the Romans in the early years of their rule. Perhaps the streams dried up? Lack of fresh water supplies? Poor harvests? Or, little or no grazing land for their cattle? All of these things forced abandonment of the established settlement to a more southerly position at "Wickham Bushes". With the help of the Romans, it became a Romano-British town.

Some of the Celts moved to an area later known as Bill Hill and Yehampstead (Easthampstead). Others went to farm at Wick Hill where there was an endless supply of water at Holy Spring. It ran downhill continually, toward Bullbrook. This kept the brook filled with water all year round. Bullbrook got its name when farmers moved their bulls and other cattle to the brook for water, then left them in fresh pastureland there.

The Romano-British settlement became quite important

as the Roman road, the Devil's Highway, bypassed the town by a mile or so. This was in direct line from the towns of Pontes (Staines) to Calleva (Silchester) on to Wickham Bushes, through to the staging post at Wokingham, near to Mathew Green Road. All the other farming settlements remained small, but later formed part and parcel of farms that would become part of Bracknell.

Roman rule brought towns and roads and work and money to the people who paid taxes to the Roman Governor. This, in turn, paid for the Army and Navy. A coin was found at Wickham Bushes in the 16th century, dated 243–245 AD to the Emperor Phillip. By then, the country was no longer a backwater, but an established part of the Roman Empire. Its capitol was at Verculum (St. Alban's), where the educated British upper class ruled in the name of Rome, and learned Latin. By 300 AD, over one and a half million people lived and worked in Britain.

In 400 AD, Roman rule was coming to an end in Britain. Slowly, the soldiers withdrew to protect Rome or other parts of the Empire. The Picts invaded from the north and the Irish from the west. Then, in 410 AD, the Roman officials decided that it was time to leave with the Army, the Navy, and the Praetorian Guard, returning to Italy. The Romano-British now had no Army or Navy to protect them, so some of the Roman towns were abandoned, like Wickham Bushes and the small staging post near to Wokingham. But the towns of Pontes and Calleva continued with reduced populations from thousands to perhaps a few hundred. So, life, of a sort, continued in the towns and rural areas until new invaders arrived who took the optimistic view that they could rule part of the Roman Empire or these islands.

From 450 AD came new invaders. Jutes, from Jutland,

near Denmark, landed in Kent, Hampshire and the Isle of Wight. Others were migrants looking for a better life from Holland, who arrived in small boats with some cattle, women and children. Others fought for every inch of land, forcing the upper class to abandon their homes, bury their gold and take what they could in the wagons to the West Country or into Wales or further north.

The Saxons soon established their rule with or without the Romano-British. They had come from Saxony in Germany and took over abandoned farms, and set up new kingdoms in Sussex, Essex, Middlesex, Surrey and Wessex. Another group was the Angles from Spitsburg Holstein, also in Germany. They killed hundreds, if not thousands, in the northern part of the country and established the kingdoms of Northumbria, Mercia and East Anglia. The Celts and the Romano-British survived in their fortified towns, but some later surrendered to the rule of the groups of invaders they called "the new race."

Anglo-Saxon Rule

This is what we think happened: The new invaders arrived and fought for land. They reoccupied the abandoned homesteads and farms, while other groups built their log cabins in or near woods, and next to streams that would become their main source of water. The Romano-British survived as the Saxons rarely were able to capture a fortified place. The British sent a letter to Rome for help. The first received a reply, but the latter did not. They realised they could not defeat the new invaders, so once the upper classes disappeared to Wales and the West Country, they decided to reoccupy most of the abandoned towns where life continued as before.

In other areas, the British ruled independently. In Wales, Cornwall, Dorset, Devon, Somerset and Columbia in the North. With a smaller population, the towns were repaired, and pottery industries continued. So, too, did the food chain and wine production. Ten years later, some Saxons arrived at the gates of the towns outnumbered five to one by the Romano-British. They allowed them to enter.

"We run the towns for the Italians," they said. "We will run them for you Germans." This was accepted and so an alderman and a small party of Saxons were left behind to take charge.

Later, they would build wooden houses around the Roman towns and those would become our modern cities of today. There is no evidence of a slaughter of the population south of the Humber. By 480 AD, more boatloads of Anglos arrived off the east coast of Britain to join people already there. The Saxons pushed the boundaries of Wessex into Berkshire and founded the towns of Reading and Windsor. Saxons and Jutes joined established farming communities of Yehampstead where they named areas where they lived as Bracken-Heal, which means Bracken and Holy by a continuous stream. This is most likely to be Holy Spring near to Wick Hill.

In the north, the Anglos pushed on but a leader of Roman origin lead the Celts to a victory in the year 500 AD at Mount-Burdon. Welsh monk and writer Guidus wrote that the battle and nine others held up the advance of the Anglos in the north for 50 years – most of his lifetime. Soon Jutes or Saxons lived under British rule in some parts of the country, even the west. Saxons gave their sons Celt names. Did they have British fathers or mothers? It begs belief, but nonetheless is true.

The two settlements became prosperous and on the site of a pre-Christian church, in 550 AD, St. Birinus set up a Celtic Christian church. The monk himself was baptised in a spring at Easthampstead located near to the church. Then, 75 years later, in 635 AD, King Cyneguis of the West Saxon kingdom dedicated the church to St. Michael and converted to the Church of Rome. It held a most prominent position on top of a hill, overlooking many farming communities. Other missionaries would pass through the area and stop to pray at the church on the hill, as it became known locally.

From 790 AD onward, Viking invaders from the coasts of Norway and Denmark began to raid south and west of the British Isles. Farmers all over the county of Berkshire would light fires in warning of the raiding Vikings. Later, in the time of King Alfred, men would train as soldiers to join his army from the parish of Bracken-Heal, and all other parishes in the great Windsor Forest, to defeat the great Viking army at a battle not far from Reading. The defeated Danes and Norwegians converted to the Christian faith and many settled as farmers in the country.

In the year 900, the first wave of Viking raids had ended. Peace was bought at a price. The name Bracken-Heal appeared on west-Saxon documents for taxation purposes, as well as on other documents and maps, as a dividing line from other villages, at the time. Such as Winfield, Warfield, Ascot-Heath and Crowthorn. Saxon, in origin, was the name Bracknell. Then, in the middle of the tenth century more raids began, but this time with large armies that wintered in an old abandoned Roman town in the north, which they partly repaired and used as their base for further attacks on other kingdoms.

By 1,000 AD, the Vikings dominated half of the country. The Kingdoms of the Anglos, Saxons' Jutes, plus the descendants of Romano-British, tried to unite the seven English kingdoms. The House of Wessex had done this already, but now tried again and was forced to give in to the Danish whose king now ruled England. After 1042 – 43 AD, the Danes were overthrown and peace came with the return of the Royal House of Wessex. Then, with the death of King Edward the Confessor, a new threat hung over the land. With no son and heir, the Council of Noblemen voted in Earl Harold Goodwin's son as king of England.

From Danish Kings to Norman Rule

So, William of Normandy landed on the south coast of England. Harold II fought and won at battle in East Anglia, an early attempt by the king of Norway to land an army capable of capturing the country, having lost his ambition. After many months of peace, the king of Norway tried again. He landed on the coast of Northumbria and marched through Yorkshire. Harold's army met them at a place called Stamford Bridge. It was said that 7,000 ships landed, but only 700 ships left that day. It was a total defeat for the Norwegian king and the end of all Viking ambitions. Now he marched south to meet William, having been told by an outrider that he had landed his army and had encamped near to Hastings. He gathered his forces as they took a slow 11 day march south from Yorkshire. The men of the Berkshire parish joined them.

Leckhampstead or Yehampstead sent five archers and the parish of Bracken-Heal sent four swordsmen to the fray. They met on October 14th and it was a total disaster for Harold and his men. Many great Englishmen died in three great battles this year of 1066 but this was to be the last. The defeated and retreated army of Harold made their way back to the hamlets and villages. Others returned to the north. William said, "Veni, vidi, vici." In English: "I came, I saw, I conquered."

William made his way around London and took the surrender of all surrounding villages there. The men of Berkshire had mostly made it back home. Prince Edgar, last of the Royal House of West Saxons, offered William the crown, which he accepted. He was crowned king of all England on Christmas Day 1066. At this time, Queen Edith held the lordship of Leckhampstead, which was worth £12 per year.

The Norman French now ruled England but wise Prince Edgar lived the rest of his life at court. He served King William plus his son and grandson. He was clever enough to outlive most of them and died in 1135, aged 85, in the reign of King Stephen. Not very much changed in the county of Berkshire until 1087 when the king's officers came to take stock of the value of the land and cattle for tax purposes which they wrote down. It's recorded in the Domesday Book, then known as Leckhampstead in the hundred of Ripplemere by the Norman officers.

Owned by King William and worth £6 before 1066, before which it was owned by Queen Edith and was worth £12. It had ten hides of land for 12 villages, with eight ploughs, and woods for 100 pigs, plus 200 head of cattle, with a total population of nearly 200 people in 1087. These would have included Binfield, Leckhampstead, Bracken-Heal and parts of Warfield and Winkfield.

Later, King William introduced the game laws of the forest to protect the deer, but William, himself, liked to hunt. He travelled to Windsor and hunted in the forest. William died fighting the King of France at Normandy. He was then succeeded by his son, Henry, whom the people of England hated. It was said, but never proven, that while out hunting one day in the New Forest of Hampshire a group of Anglo-Saxon archers fired at him. He fell and died and today a stone marks the spot. King Stephen was now king, grandson of William.

Stephen fell out with his barons and for 20 years fought a civil war against them. From 1120 onward, he began to lose and had to give in to Queen Matilda who ruled for a while before Stephen got the upper hand and Matilda fled abroad. Slowly, the barons won and Matilda returned to England. An agreement was made that Stephen could remain king until he died. Matilda's son, Henry of Anjou, would be king on Stephen's death. He was later crowned in 1135, bringing peace to England. It was also the end of the Anglo-Saxon Chronicles, week-by-week events of the country's history from 550 AD to 1135 AD.

The Middle Ages

King John began to hunt in the Windsor Forest as did late King William, realising that at the parish of Leckhampstead or Yehampstead there were thousands of acres of woodlands, ideal for hunting from August through to September. The parish was in the middle of the big towns of Windsor and Reading. As King John often paid a visit to all his lords of the manor, this was a perfect place to hunt. It was on a visit to one of his barons at Reading that he heard that there was a revolt against him by other discontented barons. He stopped at the Lodern Bridge by the river for a meal and a drink at a nearby tavern on his way to Runnymede near the old Roman town of Staines where he was forced to sign the Magna Carta (the Great Charter), a bill of rights, on the 15th of June 1215.

The bill dealt with the rights of the barons to advise the kings on matters of state, that the church was free to appoint their own priests and bishops, and that no free man shall be thrown into prison without a trial by his peers, for example those of equal status. And, that no man will be charged more than a fixed rent for his cottage and garden, etc.

John died in 1216. His son became King Henry III. He, too, was interested in hunting and became the first king to establish a small hunting lodge at the parish known as Yehampstead, where Easthampstead Park is today. The lodge and stables were built after 1238, but Henry was later captured by a knight known as "Simon de Montfort". His army forced a meeting of the first-ever parliament of England and a reissue of the Magna Carta. The lords and barons met to advise the king and the common men, who as aldermen ran the towns of England, and they should also have a say in the affairs of the state. Henry died in 1272 and Edward I became king. He, too, liked hunting, but got tied up in endless wars with Scotland and Wales. He was killed in 1307. Edward II then came to Yehampstead, but decided to alter the parish name to Easthampstead as it was east of Reading. He rebuilt the hunting lodge and employed local men to cut down some of the trees so that a path could run a few miles through the forest with marker posts so people knew their way. But he, too, became involved in wars with Scotland and Wales, which ended hunting in the forest for him. He died in 1327. Edward III would make a point of staying at Easthampstead all summer from the middle of June to late August, when he returned to London to reopen parliament.

Edward III was the first king to spend at least four months of the year at Easthampstead hunting. He ended the wars between England, Wales and Scotland, but got caught up with another war against the king of France. So, he needed parliament to vote funds to pay for a war, in return to agreement on the rights of elected members of parliament and to raise taxes. Edward died in 1377. Richard II was now crowned king and he, too, came to Easthampstead to hunt, but was tied down by wars with both France and Scotland. Easthampstead and the other parish of Bracken-Heal appeared on a map in the time of Henry IV in 1413 showing its boundaries with Binfield, Warfield, Winkfield and Crowthorn.

Neither Henry IV or V found time to hunt at Easthampstead because of the continued wars with France. The farming communities spread from Easthampstead to both sides of the church. A small manor house was built, called Manor Farm and Mill Farm. They covered an area from the church at Easthampstead to where the estates of Wild Ridings and Great Holland are today, and reached through to where the southern industrial area is today, towards Binfield. Bracknell, in the Middle Ages, may have had a population of over 400, as many cottages and farms were built and set up at this time. The only roads were the Devil's Highway and the main road that ran through from London to Reading. The next king to stay at the hunting lodge and rebuild it was Henry VI. Which he did from 1422 to 1461, until he was deposed by his barons in the Civil War, later known as the War of the Roses. Then Edward 4th was king from 1461 to 1471 and he was overthrown. Henry VI was returned to power from 1470 to 1471 when he died. Then, the Civil War brought about the return of Edward IV from 1471 to his death in 1483. Peace existed for a while but Edward V and his brother were murdered in the Tower of London, it was said, while they were asleep. Who killed them, no one knew, but Richard III was voted in as king by parliament. After, he turned down the crown twice. He may not have been responsible for the murders, but could it have been someone of a rival house of Lancaster who put the blame on Richard?

Richard only stayed at the lodge in the spring of 1484, but another rebellion by the Lancastrians was on the cards. Lord Stanley promised support, so at Market Bosworth in Lincolnshire the armies met. Lord Stanley changed sides. Richard fell from his horse and was killed on the 22nd of August 1485. It became known as the battle that ended the Middle Ages.

The Tudors

As the hunting lodge and stables were not used at Easthampstead Park during the War of the Roses, they were now in urgent need of repair, so Henry VII decided to have the whole hunting lodge and stables pulled down. In order to rebuild the whole place, he decided to build a large manor house on the site and assembled a skilled workforce of about 100 men to build the house for him. Stonemasons, carpenters and all other tradesmen were found. He decided to have stables and rooms for servants, then employed gardeners to landscape and plant out the grounds. He had a long driveway built that lead to a road that went to Crowthorn or Wokingham, then he had a road made so that he could travel from London to Easthampstead, then to the new house and its park.

It took three years. He got all the local men he could, but bought other skills from London to help complete the work. By the time it was completed in 1493, he had quarters for all his servants and new stables were built. He had 300 acres of gardens and hundreds of acres of woodland to hunt in. Henry enjoyed the hunt now he had thousands of acres of woods to hunt in and ten miles of pathways to travel along.

Henry died suddenly in 1509 and his son became king as Henry VIII. Henry would carry out his father's work by adding a new road from Ascot to Easthampstead Park that would pass by local farms such as Manor Farm, Mill Farm, Northern and Peacock Farms. Then, the new road would continue on to the new Easthampstead Park and continue to Wokingham or Crowthorn. Henry's son, Arthur the Prince of Wales, who had arranged a marriage for his father to Catherine of Aragon, rode out to meet her and her party at Finchampstead Ridges. She later married Henry but spent some long miserable years in exile at the park until a divorce was agreed, then Henry's attentions turned to Anne Boleyn. Sir John Mason was keeper of the park from 1503 to 1566, when the estate was enlarged. Catherine then received her messengers from the king about the divorce at the park. The park was kept well-stocked with deer, so that Henry could go there any time he wanted, with or without his wives. Henry died in London aged just 56 in 1547.

After Henry died, his son, who became Edward VI, had no interest in hunting, just affairs of State. After only six years, he became ill and died. His sister, Mary, became queen and kept the Tudors in power. She married the king of Spain and was in charge of England, so prevented war. Mary did visit Easthampstead Park a few times but didn't take part in hunting. Mary died in 1558. The Lords and Commons then voted for a Tudor to take the throne and promptly sent King Phillip of Spain back home. He thought that his marriage to Mary Tudor entitled him to be King of England but the people and parliament had other ideas. So, Elizabeth Tudor became queen. She sent Captains Drake and Hawkins around the world to explore. Something the Spanish, Portuguese and Italians had been doing for some time with the discovery of America and the Great Renaissance. This was an English Golden Age.

Elizabeth stayed many times at Easthampstead Park and took part in hunting. She liked to ride through the great Windsor Forest. It was during the Elizabethan era that one tenant farmer, William Twig, farmed around Northern Farm and the Millpond area of Bracknell, which is now the Great Holland's Estate. It was in early 1973 that my brother Colin Clark found a coin while planting a tree with co-workers Phillip Inkwell and Ted Butler. It was dated 1668 and found in a road known as Wordsworth, proof that William Twig or someone dropped a coin here. In searching the local church parish death records, I could find no trace of him. He may have died in another parish. After Drake and Hawkins defeated the Spanish in 1588, Elizabeth would pass through the parish of Bracken-Heal and others on her way to Easthampstead Park where she would stay in residence every summer until she died in 1603.

The Stuarts and the Civil War

One thing all kings and queens of the Middle Ages liked about Easthampstead Park was the water from the well. It was said to have healing properties with chalybeate or mineral water. This was impregnated with iron. It also cured eye troubles. The well was situated on the Ludgrove Estate, then known as Luckley Estate. Most importantly, the well was filled in in the early part of the 20th century.

James I stayed at the park from 1605 onward. He enjoyed the gardens and would spend most of the summer hunting in the forest with a family called the Trumbulls, who had served the king at the court of the Archduke Albert of Austria in the Netherlands from 1609 to 1625. In 1625, the park was given to the Trumbull family for their service to the crown. They would provide 200 deer for the king's recreation, which they did for all kings up to the Civil War. During the war and afterwards, the Trumbulls were still recognised as the lord of the manor but kept a low profile until Charles II was restored to the throne.

A later royal charter confirmed the gift of the park to

the Trumbull family. This was dated March 28th 1629. The charter was thought to have been lost but later found in London and has been purchased by the Berkshire record office. Sir William Trumbull, 1639 to 1716, was active in the Royal Service overseas. He was also a fellow of All Souls College, Oxford and a barrister. He became friends with poet Alexander Pope, who lived in Binfield and was a frequent visitor to the park. Another poet, Elijah Fenton, was the tutor to William Trumbull IV, 1708 to 1760. His only child, Mary Trumbull, married Martin Sandys in 1760. Then their only child, Mary Sandys, married Arthur Hill the second Marquess of Downshire from 1753 to 1801. She was made Baroness Sandys in 1786.

Easthampstead Park

Mary Sandys, from 1764 to 1836, lived most of her life at the park with the second Marquess of Downshire. The Trumbull manuscripts were inherited by the family. There are some 380 volumes of them, mostly letters to the Stuart kings, to Phillip II of Spain, Marie de Medici, and to poets and writers of the era: Bacon, Dryden, Donne, Pope and Fenton. They were on loan to the Berkshire records office, then the collection went to Sotheby's in London. The auction was later cancelled, so the British Library took the papers. Arthur Hill succeeded as the second Marquess of Downshire upon the death of his father, William. In 1793, he began the building of Hillsborough Castle in Northern Ireland that was completed in 1797. Arthur Hill and Mary had five sons.

The first son was Arthur Blundell Sandys Trumbull Hill, the third Marquess of Downshire, who lived from 1788 to 1845. During this time, there was some rebuilding of the Manor House and the gardens were extended. The park covered over 300 acres of land. This was not counting the thousands of acres of woodlands that were still used for hunting by the family and by most kings and queens up until the end of the Stuart era. During the 17th and 18th centuries, other rich families came to live in Bracknell, or the old parish of Easthampstead, so new large manor houses were built at this time. South Hill Park built in 1780, Wick Hill House built in 1800, and Lily Hill House built in 1807, whose grounds and gardens covered part of Bullbrook and Harman's Water.

The other sons were Arthur Moyses William Hill, 2nd Baron Sandys from 1793 to 1860. Arthur Marcus Cecil Sandys, 3rd Baron Sandys from 1798 to 1863. Then Arthur August Edwin Sandys from 1800 to 1831. The fifth son was Major Lord George August Sandys from 1801 to 1879. In a letter to Mrs Russell of Thornhill dated May 1857, she wrote to Jane Carlyle the wife of Thomas Carlyle, whose friend Lady Ashburton had recently died of influenza, "I am going to Easthampstead Park to see the Marquess of Downshire, to stay for a while. Almost immediately, those great country manor houses are not the place nature prompts me to when I am sick or of bad spirits, when I am going as a sort of irresponsible carpetbagger, with Mr Carlyle's name on it. It's hoping my ill health will pass and I will feel the joys of spring again."

Easthampstead was only one of the properties of the Marquesses. Their large estate in Northern Ireland was one of 115,000 acres. The forth Marquess confusingly called himself Arthur William Blundell Sandys Trumbull Windsor Hill, 1812 to 1868. In 1860, major repair works and extensions were being carried out and were not completed until 1864. The family also paid for repairs to St. Michael's church. Here there are memorials to the Trumbull and Downshire families, and also the poet Elijah Fenton. In 1885, King Edward VII paid a visit to the park and he too enjoyed the hunting in the forest.

The Downshires were active in Northern Ireland, and the sixth Marquess (1871 to 1918) lived all his life there. During Ascot week he would return to the park and employ hundreds of local men to work in the grounds and gardens and help at the hunt. He also had a steam roller to help in the upkeep of the roads. He built a miniature steam railway within the park grounds. He kept the gardens well-stocked with rare and diverse species of exotic plants and trees.

After the First World War, the roads were built around the park from Ascot to Bracknell, and roads to Crowthorn and Wokingham. Then, after the last owner died in 1936, the next Marquess of Downshire was more interested in his lands in Ireland. He sold the park to the Berkshire County Council after the end of World War II. During the war, the St. Paul's school was evacuated from London to Easthampstead Park. The school also used the playing fields of Wellington College. Then, in 1941 the Germans bombed the driveway as the British Army had used the grounds and forest as a training centre.

Then, as I have said, the park was sold. In 1946, there was a fire, so the Berkshire County Council and the insurance company paid for repairs and major restoration to the manor house. In 1949, it became a teacher training college run by the Council, until 1970 when the park became a major conference centre for local firms and companies.

Late 17th Century to Georgian Era

From the latter 17th century, taverns or inns began appearing in what would become Bracknell High Street. The Hind's Head was the first of many built in 1650 on a site where the modern Bracknell College now stands. It was a place where a weary traveller could get a bath, bed, a meal or a beer. Nearby was another large manor house built in the early 1600s called The Old Manor. Down the road, was yet another tavern or inn called The Crown that stood on the site where the post office now stands.

The first shops appeared at the end of the 17th century. A wheel wrights shop, a cobblers and a blacksmiths all stood at the top of the high street. A tobacconists would have been popular at this time. The parishes of Bracknell and Easthampstead and other hamlets or villages later added to the working population. By 1711, more taverns had been built. The Prince of Wales, The Bull and The Red Lion were all popular with local people and had a good trade of travellers passing through the town on stagecoaches.

Kelly's Directory, a kind of 18th century yellow pages,

noted that Bracknell's taverns had 15 beds for travellers, and stables for 25 horses. One tavern, The Crown, was so popular that some travellers from afar never returned. When, in 1760, the landlord sold The Crown and moved to London, it was said that the wells were blocked, so men were paid to clear them but found the remains of six missing people from as many counties. Six skeletons were removed and the well filled in, and another source of water was found. In 1765, the landlord and his wife were later traced by the authorities, arrested, sent for trial and hanged together in 1765 at Reading Jail.

Soon, more wealthy families arrived in the village and more manor houses were built. South Hill Park in 1780, Wickhill House in 1790 and Lily Hill House by 1800. The first census was taken in 1801, and 386 people lived in Bracknell Village, but kings still came to Easthampstead Park to hunt. George I and II both enjoyed hunting most summers while staying at the park. It was said of George III that he once chased a stag throughout the forest for four hours or even five, but still it got away. This was in 1781, but he returned to complete more rides through the forest. The queen, it was said, would ride all day covering some 40 miles, then got lost and returned to the park just as it got dark.

The 18th century was a time of pirates and highwaymen, who had their base in Blackwater, but were known to frequent the taverns of both Bracknell and Wokingham. The Hind's Head was a favourite place to drink or hide and grease the palm of the landlord with silver coins and he would gladly lead the authorities to a dead end. Time enough for the highwaymen to escape down some secret tunnel to another part of the village and away on the fastest horses to the next town and tavern. George IV came to the park and hunted in the forest, but one afternoon took a bad fall from his horse. He was brought home to the park to rest and a doctor was sent for. He sent him to bed and said, "Just a few cuts and bruises, nothing broken." The king returned to Windsor and when he was fit enough would return to hunt again.

The census of 1811 showed that Bracknell had a population of 423 people. Most worked on farms but with the ever-growing manor houses, many would have been servants, estate gardeners, carpenters or blacksmiths. Others would have worked in the taverns, inns or shops. The main turnpike roads were the London to Reading road that passed through Bracknell and Wokingham. The second major new road was the forest turnpike that went from Wokingham through the villages of Wokingham without Binfield, Warfield and Winfield toward Windsor.

By the 1821 census, the population seemed to stabilise at 442 people. After the death of George IV, the Downshire family invited the new King William IV to a grand ball and dinner at the park. It was a two day event plus entertainment then the hunt. The king had such a great time, he often corresponded with the Downshires once a month, perhaps hoping for more invites to balls, dinners and hunting.

The Victorian Era

In the census of 1831, Bracknell was still a small village with a population of almost 500 people. Queen Victoria became queen in 1837 and would come to Ascot every day of the week. She would also visit the Duke of Wellington, who lived in a village some miles north of Reading. In 1845, she was late arriving to see the Duke of Wellington, so she sent word by a messenger that she would be late. The driver of the stagecoach, due to bad weather, decided to stop in a village called Bracknell at the tavern known as The Red Lion, to rest overnight, have a meal, a beer or two or coffee. The horses were taken to the stables for the night. It was good accommodation for the queen and her servants but they were underway early the next day.

Soon things were to change in Bracknell for the Staines line through to Reading arrived in 1854 to 1856 with the coming of the railway. There was work for local men in Bracknell and the surrounding villages. More people came to live and work there. The 1841 census showed 542 people living in Bracknell. By the 1851 census, the population grew to almost 600 and by 1871, it had reached 721. The railway brought more people, so more shops were built in the high street. In 1859, a new church was built in the high street. Then, in 1867 Bracknell became a parish in its own right with the building of the Holy Trinity Church.

In 1861, one of my ancestors decided to come to the Bracknell area for a job, found lodgings and a girlfriend. They had a relationship and on July the 10th 1862, she gave birth to my two times great-grandfather, George Clark. The baby's father David Clark left and abandoned his child after 18 months and returned to Reading. George grew up in a children's home but in 1878 he married Louise Young, a lady from Warfield. In 1875, the Hobleys from Oxford came to live in Bracknell, Thomas Hobley was a local wheelwright at Warfield and Bracknell villages.

South Hill Park

South Hill Park was built in 1760 by William Watts, who lived there when he retired from the Indian civil service in Bengal. The park was set in 300 acres of woods and gardens. After the death of William Watts, the property was bought by the Honourable Henry Bouverie, whose family lived in the house until his death in 1787. He was followed by Sir Stephen Lushington, who owned it in 1807, then it was bought by George Canning, who was later chancellor under William Pitt, the younger, but became prime minister later. He loved the gardens and would invite important people in society down for balls and dinner parties. King William, Victoria's father, was one important visitor.

George Canning died in 1827 when the house passed to Sir John Soane, who became the owner of the house. He had the place rebuilt and modified. The next owners were the Earls of Limerick. It was said that they, too, enjoyed the gardens and employed a dozen or so local men to look after the gardens and as many servants to run the house. In Kelly's Directory of 1847, it is stated that James Matheson was in residence. After this, the house was sold in 1853 to Sir William Goodenough Hayter. He was the son of the Judge Advocate General of the United Kingdom. In 1868, South Hill Park was referred to in Kelly's Directory as one of the nicest mansions in the parish of Easthampstead.

Sir William, it would seem, had a busy career that later made him depressed. He was found dead at South Hill Park's lake. Lady Hayter then became the next owner. It was again mentioned in Kelly's Directory in 1883 as a lovely house set in 800 acres of gardens and woodlands. Sir William's son was Sir Arthur Divett Hayter, born in 1835. He lived most of his life at South Hill Park. He paid the architect Temple Moore, 1856 to 1920, to re-landscape most of the gardens near to the house. He made a very good job of the gardens and most of his work can still be seen today. Sir Arthur became Baron Haversham in 1906, after which Haversham Drive is named. They kept a large staff at the park. At one time, over 100 people were employed as estate carpenters, gardeners, blacksmiths and general servants. Sadly, Lord Haversham died on the 10th of May 1917 and Lady Haversham lived at the house until 1920. She had a marble tablet made as a memorial to all the men who had lost their lives in the First World War, and had it placed at Easthampstead Church.

Lady Haversham died at the house in 1929. Her nephew had inherited the house and he was Major Rickman OBE. And so became the last owner of South Hill Park. The major had money troubles and mounting debts. In 1940, he took his own life and was found dead in the gunroom. The family rented the house to the Royal Sea Bathing Hospital, who occupied the house from 1941 to 1945 when they returned to Margate where they had been evacuated from. The house was then sold to the BBC in 1946. By 1953, the BBC had converted the rooms into flats and studios, then it was rented to Ferranti as offices until 1972 when the Bracknell Development Corporation bought the house and used it as an arts centre with flats, offices and restored gardens. In 1973, the South Hill Park trust was set up and a theatre built at the side of the old house which opened in 1984. It was called the Wilde Theatre after the famous Irish playwright and poet, Oscar Wilde.

The Victorian Bracknell Town

1837	Victoria became queen of United Kingdom of Great Britain. Civil registration began, all persons born from now on, must have a birth or death certificate and be registered within 30 days, marriages to be recorded by the local register.
1845	Queen Victoria stayed overnight at The Red Lion in Bracknell High Street.
1854	Coming of the railway to Staines line through to Reading.
1856	Completion of the railway link.
1861	The census, 589 people in Bracknell.
1862	Birth of George Clark, my two times great-grandfather.
1865	A large manor house built at Priestwood, later known as the Admiral Cunningham. Another large manor house was built near to Bullbrook, known as Ramslade house.
1871	The census, 723 people living in Bracknell.

1878	Marriage of George Clark to Louise Young at a church in Binfield.
1880	Six cottages built in Binfield Road and eight houses built at Downshire Way. The owner of Woodside House at Wokingham Road had three sets of cottages built for his servants. They were known as Mays Cottage, Fairview and Horthern Cottages.
1881	Building of one large house and six smaller houses at Stoney Road. The census, 857 people living in Bracknell.
1882	Opening of Thomas and Sons Brickworks at Warfield, employing many local men.
1884	Birth of my great-grandfather Thomas Clark, son of George and Louise Clark.
1885	Edward VII stayed at Easthampstead Park.
1891	The census, 1,127 people now lived in Bracknell.
1892	More houses built in Bracknell at London Road, near to Priestwood Common and in Bullbrook. George Clark and family moved from Jellots Hill to Bullbrook, renting a house owned by the Berkshire County Council. He became a stationary steam engine driver at Bracknell Station.
1894	Opening of the new public houses, the Railway Tavern and the Bricklayer Arms.
1897	The Queen's Diamond Jubilee.
1900	Opening of Tile and Brick Company, known as the Binfield Brickworks, at Longshot Lane. Marriage of Thomas Clark to Edith Neale.

Lily Hill House

The Lily Hill Park and its woods date back to 1761. The site of the house was built and purchased by Henry Dormer Vincent, Esq. He was the second son of the MP for Surrey and in 1807, when the house was completed, he moved in. The house and its park first appeared on a local map in 1817. After his death in 1833, it passed to his eldest son, Henry William Vincent. He was aged just 37 at the time of his inheritance and was working for the Exchequer in the Judicial, a post known as the King and Queen's Remembrancer. It was Henry William Vincent who designed much of the gardens without help of any professional assistance. Henry consulted with his friends from Eton school, one being Ralph Sneyd of Staffordshire, who had undertaken similar work.

In 1865, Henry William Vincent died. His eldest daughter Susan Ann Bagot Lane was now the owner of the house. After Susan's death in 1899, the estate was sold by public auction, so Lily Hill House left the Vincent family. In 1902, Charles Neck bought it but died in 1904, after which the house was held in trustee of the estate.

In 1912, Mrs Charles Neck sold the house to Jennings Scott McComb and moved to London. By 1928, Mrs Mary Scott McCombs inherited the house following her husband's demise. After her death in 1955, the family sold the house to the Bracknell Development Corporation, who used the house as offices then rented them out. They restored most of the park and gardens. In 1983, after the disbanding of the Bracknell Development Corporation, the ownership of the house, park and gardens went to the Bracknell Forest Borough Council, who funded the completed restoration of the house and gardens over the next ten years. The house was eventually sold to a private owner, but the Council still manages the park and gardens.

Wick Hill House

Wick Hill House at Bracknell was built in the early 1800s and is a nice country manor house. It was once the house of George Littledale, who bought the house in 1895 and lived there until his death in 1931. He was a game hunter who collected for museums. He was born in Liverpool in 1851 and his parents were Thomas Littledale and Julia Royds. His father and grandfather were wealthy cotton brokers. He collected birds and mammals. He sailed around the world and even honeymooned in the Kashmir. He married in 1877 to Teresa Scott and their travels took them to North America, Asia, Russia, and later to Outer Mongolia by 1897. In 1893, they crossed into China and Tibet. The Royal Geographical Society awarded him a Patron's Medal for his three expeditions. His wife died suddenly in 1928 and George then kept a low profile at Wick Hill House until he died there in 1931.

The Edwardians and the Great War

1901   January 22nd death of Queen Victoria. Her son Albert was now king as Edward VII. In 1901, the tow brick and tile companies at Warfield and Longshot Lane were the only industries in Bracknell. Everyone was employed as farm estate workers for the gentry and servants for building companies. The census, 2,372 people living in Bracknell.

1902   Ramslade House was owned by Colonel McKenzie who was a retired Army officer. He lived in the house from the late 1890s to 1940.

1903   The birth of Sidney Thomas Hobley, my grandfather, at Mount Pleasant. Also in this year, a retired civil servant from India Septimus smet Thornburn, bought Bracknell house in the old Bracknell Lane. He lived there from 1903 to his death in 1913. The house was then bought by Harold Footman

	OBE, who lived there throughout the 1930s.
1904	Mr Strachan set up the first motor garage in the town, also Mr Graves, a coal merchant, began operation from his cottage Puddleduck Cottage in the London Road.
1905	The Fletcher brothers set themselves up as grocers in London Road. Arthur Atkins set up a boot and shoemakers that ran from 1903 to 1916, also in London Road.
1906–1907	The Forest Hotel was a very popular place to stay and dine in Bracknell at prices only the rich could afford. The Admiral Cunningham was still a private house, but by 1954 it was a public house.
1908	Bertie Bickmore, a blacksmith, came to Bracknell with his family. They lived at 1 Fairview Cottages along the Wokingham Road.
1911	Alfred Young opened a saddler in Station Road. After 1918, he was selling boots and shoes. By 1950, he had a tobacconist shop in the high street.
1914	August 4th was the start of a war that was to last over four years and cost the lives of some 15 million people. A war they called a world war.
1915	Mr Twidell had begun manufacturing bicycles in the Wokingham Road. He later opened a shop in the high street after the war.

Mid-Twentieth Century

1918   Ceasefire on southern and western fronts from November 11th. Thomas Clark went to buy a newspaper and read that the war was over. Celebrations took place all day in Bracknell. His son, Sidney Clark, who was wounded and spent two months in a French hospital, returned home in early December 1918.

1919–1920 Easthampstead Rural Council built fourteen council houses at Binfield Road for men returning from the war and their families.

1920–1921 Building of new houses at Easthampstead Road, Stoney Road, Green Lane, Clay Lane and Skipped Hill Lane. 1921 census, 3,894 people in Bracknell.

1922   Bracknell was now recognised as a town, no longer referred to as a village on maps.

1923   A war memorial was erected at St. Michael's Church in Easthampstead.

1927	The birth of Dorothy Hobley, whose father, Sidney Hobley, lived at Broad Lane.
1928	Death of Teresa Littledale at Wick Hill House.
1929	Marriage of Albert Ernest Sidney Clark to Maude Bickmore, who was the daughter of Bertie Bickmore, a local blacksmith.
1930	Birth of Bernard Sidney Thomas Clark, my father, to parents Maude and Sidney Clark.
1931	Death of George Littledale at Wick Hill House. The census, 4,620 people in Bracknell.
1932–1933	Over 900 men were out of work in the Bracknell District. Electrical power station was built in Western and Easthampstead Roads.
1934	Demolition of The Crown public house, which was replaced by a modern post office. A stone was placed inside the church at Easthampstead in memory of the 62 men of Bracknell who died in the Great War. More new houses were built at Rounds Hill, plus a new shop was built there.
1935	Local schools in Bracknell were Bullbrook, opened in 1866, Ranelagh, opened in 1770, Sandy Lane, opened in 1885, and Priestwood School, opened in 1908. Three of the schools were taken over by Berkshire County Council. Court records for 1936 showed one Frederick Broadway, known as Sparrow Broadway, as he had narrow legs, was a trainer of dogs, building site worker and poacher who got caught and sent to the local magistrate's

court. The magistrate was his old Colonel Barker from the Berkshire regiment who had fought in the First World War. "You are a disgrace to the regiment," he said. Broadway said, "Yes, sir." He was fined five shillings then the colonel paid his fine for him after asking if he was free on Sunday for the hunt. The Colonel thought a lot of old Sparrow, it was said. He had a way with dogs and used to drink at the old Prince of Wales in the high street. Kelly's Trade Directory of 1936 lists the following firms in Bracknell: Lawrence Stores, Mathesons Carpet Fitters, James William Maidmert Boot and Shoemaker, Arthur Martin Newsagents at Binfield Road, Edith Maynard Tobacconist, Frank Millard Corn and Flour Merchants, Harry Noyes Grocer and Post Office, John Pinnell Baker at the Station, a wireless engineer, the Co-op, Mr Youens Cycle Repair Shop and Mr Carter Coal Merchants.

1937   More building of houses at Easthampstead and Binfield Roads, down to the junction of Stoney Road.

1939   Death of George Clark, start of World War II when all men aged 18–42 were called up under the Military Service Act.

1940   The RAF won the Battle of Britain, forcing Hitler to cancel his invasion of Great Britain.

1942   Death of Louise Clark, wife of George Clark, a local steam engine driver.

1943   The war turned in favour of the western allies

and Russia. Wednesday the 10th of February, the only raid on Reading in World War II, over 100 people were killed or injured. The landlord of the Leather and Bottle at Barkham Wokingham was killed but his wife and daughter survived. The home guard shot down a German plane at Sonning Common. The crew spent the rest of the War at Reading prison.

1944   D-Day landings by the western allies were successful. The attack on Germany by a wide front from south to the west and north. Russia and its eastern allies attack from the east.

1946   Easthampstead Rural Council built 60 new houses at Skimped Hill.

1949   The Bracknell Development Corporation was set up to build a new town with its headquarters at Farley Hall.

1950   Bernard Clark married Dorothy May Hobley and moved into 1 Fairview Cottages, Wokingham Road, near Bracknell.

1951   Bernard Clark took photos of the first houses built opposite his cottage along Wokingham Road. The census, 5,253.

1953   Over 1,000 houses built at Priestwood Common, the first phase of the new town with parks and open spaces. Birth of Terry John Clark.

After World War II

Firms and shops in the high street at the start of the new town in 1950, according to Kelly's Directory: the Royal Foresters Hotel, W.T. Stevens Ironmongers, Spinning Wheel Café, the International Stores, Sirls Furnishers, Mathesons Carpet Fitters, W.A. Green Ironmongers, J.W. Smiths Newsagents, the Home Colonial Butchers, Timothy Whites, Cheneys Newsagents and Confectionery.

March the 11th 1950, death of my great-grandfather, Bertie Bickmore, who had worked and lived in the town from 1908 to 1950. He was a blacksmith by trade and fought in the First World War, where he rose to the rank of Company Sergeant Major. The building of the new town began in early 1951 and the first residents to move in to the area once known as Priestwood Common were in by Christmas. Over 1,000 houses were built there over the next two years. By 1954, the population had grown by 2,500, with new houses with electricity and running water, parks, open spaces and shops, and industrial areas where work could be found. The area became a popular place to live and work.

By 1954, building works had started at Easthampstead for another 1,000 houses. This was mostly completed by 1955 when building began at Bullbrook. In 1954, the Armorial Cunningham was sold and became a public house. The old Prince of Wales in the high street was pulled down, but rebuilt at Priestwood. At Bullbrook, the stream was piped in and the brook drained. Some houses were pulled down in the London Road. Western and eastern industrial areas had now been built and completed providing work for people moving into the area. By the time Harman's Water was completed in 1959-1960, the population stood at 15,327, a rise in ten years of 10,000 plus people who came to live in Bracknell.

1956	Death of great-grandmother, Emma Louise Bickmore.
1957	Birth of my brother, Colin Roy Clark.
1958	Terry John Clark started school at Priestwood.
1959	Demolition of the Foresters Hotel in the high street.
1960	Phase one of the new town is completed with almost 17,000 people in the town.
1961	It was decided by the government to expand the town at Bracknell, towards the north.

In 1959, the corporation pulled down Woodside House and the original Bridge House pub that stood along the Wokingham Road. The house disappeared for good, but the public house was rebuilt on the opposite side of the road. In their place was built Rascal's and Dorothy Perkins but all houses either side of Rounds Hill survived. In 1960, new shops opened at the Broadway and the Crossway.

A bypass was built around the town and extending roads were improved or extended to make way for extra traffic. By 1961, phase one of the town was completed. A government minister decided to enlarge the town so the corporation issued CPO orders for some of the lands north of the town, from Manor Farm to Mill Farm, perhaps Home Farm. Those areas were to become the future estates of Wild Ridings and Great Hollands, plus the new southern industrial area.

A new school was built in the town. The first was Meadowvale and Wick Hill secondary. At Priestwood, Sandy Lane was rebuilt and enlarged. Fox Hill primary in Easthampstead Bracken-Heal, also at Easthampstead, and Harman's Water primary...all built from 1954-1958. In 1962, a road accident outside 1 Fairview Cottages wrote off my father's car which was parked outside, but ended up 16 yards up the road with another car. 1963 saw the death of my great-grandmother, Edith Clark née Neale, and the coldest winter for 200 years. The temperature never rose above freezing for the 31 days of January, and the Beatles became very popular overnight. By March, the snow and frost had gone and the daffodils were out, spring was here at last.

1962	My brother Colin started at Priestwood School.
1963	My great-uncle, Frank Clark, began working as a carpet fitter at Matheson's.
1964	After the tile and brick company packed up in the winter of 1963-1964, the area became three lakes for fisherman, and woods for kids to play in.

| 1965 | The Hind's Head was demolished to make way for Bracknell College. The cattle market was moved to Market Street and the good market was relocated to the rear of The Red Lion public house. |

In 1966, phase two of the town began. Wild Riding was to become the fifth new estate in Bracknell to be built on lands bought by the corporation from the owners of Manor Farm. The estate reached Easthampstead Church and was completed in 1968. The corporation left 15 acres of land at Manor Farm as the rest was used for building. In what became the southern industrial area, this required the disappearance of Mill Farm, but the lake and the woods were saved and management of them turned into a park by Bracknell Town Council.

In 1967, a start was made on the biggest corporation project yet...the building of the town's biggest estate of some 3,000 houses. It was not completed until 1971, but the first residents moved in in early 1969.

1966	England won the World Cup (football).
1967	The Clark family moved from Bracknell, having been there since 1861 and occupied Fairview Cottage since 1908.
1968	Colin Clark began secondary education at St. Crispin's school.
1969	Terry Clark left school and began work for the Bracknell Development Corporation.
1970	The corporation began a process of complete demolition of the old Bracknell high street, not completed until 1972.

1971	Charles Square opened with new shops and the whole high street was rebuilt, only the Old Manor, the house next to the manor, and the other public houses...The Red Lion, The Bull and Gingers...were the only buildings to survive the demolition. The census, 23,124 people living in Bracknell. A rise of about 12,000 since 1961.
1972	The town's high street was completed and had lots of new shops but not many of the old families running shops came back. Most retired or moved to the surrounding villages.
1973	The corporation started on the final phase of the town. The sudden death of my grandparents, Albert Ernest Sidney Clark, then two days later in Binfield, the death of his wife, Maude Else Clark, née Bickmore.
1973–1974	Work began on what would become the Birch Hill and Hanworth estates. More demolition of old houses in the town at Stanley Road and Church Road. Stanley Road was named after Lord and Lady Stanley, who owned a large house at the junction of Holy Spring Lane and Park Road. When they died in 1969, someone set fire to the house. It was saved but badly damaged. Relations in South Africa were traced and the house and grounds sold to the corporation who built a small housing estate on the site. All that remains is the large wall that surrounded the estate. The disappearance of Victoria Road and Hall and more houses here. The same happened

in London Road, Bagshot Road and Mount Pleasant.

1975–1976   Demolition of all houses at Easthampstead Road. Mrs Dee was the last to move as her husband died the year before.

My father's old cottage was built in 1880 and our family lived there from 1908 to 1967 (1 and 2 Fairvew Cottages). They were pulled down in 1976 (13th of August). That year, Mr Cooper had moved from Mays Cottages to Faircross. His old property was knocked down the same month; only one survivor was Hawthorn Cottages that were still occupied to the end of 1978 when this, too, was pulled down. The area was cleared and became a carpark for Rascal's for the next 20 years. By 1976 to 1977, the corporation had completed most of the third stage of the new town, as people moved into Birch Hill and Hanworth estates. The ninth and final estate was the Queen's Crown Estate. With it, the corporation had completed its job for which it had been set up in 1959, to build a modern new town at Bracknell.

So the corporation began to disband, transferring its staff of landscape gardeners and all building trades over to the local council, the Easthampstead Rural Council was now known as Bracknell District Council. From 1971 to 1979, all staff including managers, supervisors and general office staff, from middle management, were working for the local council. The census of 1981, the population of the new town stood at 31,340 people. The corporation ended and disbanded in 1983 and the last staff were made redundant. Farley Hall has remained empty ever since (30 years), this would have made an ideal place for a Bracknell hospital.

After 1983, there was not much going on as building projects go until 1988 when it was decided to redevelop the western and eastern industrial areas. Over the next four years, all of the office blocks and factories built in the 1950s were completely replaced with ultra-modern buildings. At Wokingham Road, the cottages of Mays, Fairview and Horthorn had long since been demolished. Now, the site was redeveloped at Trinity Court. This concluded with the replacement of Rascal's and Dorothy Perkins buildings.

In Easthampstead Road, where the houses came down for the extension of Clifford's dairies, now that Mr Clifford had died, the properties were sold and redeveloped as Homebase on one side of the road, with a new company taking over the other side for an office block and park. The old Sperry's site, too, saw a multi-office complex built with a park and hotel.

Then from 1990, the Qualm Park private building development began. This was within the town's boundaries and where Binfield once was, a half mile away, just across the road to the golf course, less than 100 yards away. This boosted up the population once more. The 1991 census had the population count of Bracknell Town at 41,354, yet another ten-year increase in the population. Slowing down on previous decades, but still going up. The 1992 to 1994 development north of Bracknell saw 3,000-4,000 houses stay on the Warfield boundary, but Bullbrook was now yards away, not miles. Other building projects concentrated on Binfield, Warfield and Crowthorn, and other parts of the country. Bracknell once was an obscure and unknown town, until a war-time minister found it on the map and decided that, after the war, it would make a great new town. Now a well-known and ultra-modern town within the county of Berkshire. By 2001, the census showed a slowing down in the increasing Bracknell population to 45,756. After 2003, the local council had considered knocking down and rebuilding the Broad and Crossway, but these are projects of the future.

Postscript

Local men who died in the First or Second World Wars:

Private H.L. Williams
Captain J. Connell
Lance Corporal A. Gibbs
Private G. Fage
RN L. Lewer
C.A. Emmerrick
Home Guard E. Higgs
Private Gordon Clark
RAF Sergeant R.E. Browne
Army Driver G. White
RN D.C.H. Lassam
2nd Lieutenant T.G. Evans
W.A.F. Joy Burton
Royal Marine S. Srangege
Army A.J Charters
Private A. Norris
RAF W.D. Parry
Sergeant J. Bidwell

Some local men who survived both wars to tell their
stories to me:

Company Sergeant Major Bertie Augustus Bickmore
Army Arthur Woods
RN Frank William Cooper
Army Arthur Sylvester
Staff Sergeant Albert Ernest Sidney Clark
RAF Ken Inns
Army Philip Inkwell
Army Edward Butler
Army Medic John Soman
Army Eric Evans
Army Charley Binge
Sergeant Frederick Vass
Army Denis Norris

Lily Hill House 1880
© Bracknell Central Library

George Canning 1881
Photo courtesy of Patricia Brombley

Bracknell High Street 1907
© Sanda Chin

Bracknell 1910
Photo courtesy of Patricia Brombley

Church Road 1910
Photo courtesy of Patricia Brombley

Frank Hobley 1918
Photo courtesy of Sidney Hobley

George Littledale 1920
Photo courtesy of Patricia Brombley

Berti Bickmore and Bernard S T Clark 1933
Photo courtesy of Colin Clark

Easthampstead Park 1936
© Bracknell Central Library

Old Bracknell c1950
Photo courtesy of Dorothy May Clark

New town houses 1951
Photo courtesy of Bernard S T Clark

Hinds Head pub 1965
Photo courtesy of Bernard S T Clark

Sidney Thomas Hobley 2003
Photo courtesy of Colin Clark

Wick Hill House 2011
Photo courtesy of Terry Clark